THE VACATION SCHEME, TRAINING CONTRACT APPLICATIONS TINY HANDBOOK

TEMPLATES TO STRUCTURE COMMERCIAL LAW WRITTEN ANSWERS

LEO MILES

Version 1.0

For enquiries, contact the author through email:
leomilesbooks@mail.com

For all those friends who are chasing their dreams.

CONTENTS

PREFACE

Hello! Thanks for picking up *The Vacation Scheme, Training Contract Applications Tiny Handbook*.

This book will help you understand what to focus on when answering the most common application questions for commercial law vacation schemes and training contracts. The insights you will learn come directly from successful applicants and conversations with graduate recruitment and solicitors.

While students usually understand what to include in their answers, they often struggle to grasp how to present their experiences and structure their answers in a clear and concise manner.

But that high level of writing skill is precisely what law firms are looking for.

By this point in your preparation, you should already know that you need to back up all your statements with clear evidence, such as examples and numbers.

WEAK EXAMPLE: I understand the value of teamwork.

STRONGER EXAMPLE: I drafted cold calling scripts

and led a team of twenty-five students as the Vice President of the Midnight Kayaking Society to meet our £10,000 fundraising goal.

But so many students follow these tips and are still rejected at the application stage. So, what is the issue?

It comes down to **two key factors**:

1. Your Extracurriculars: Who are you beyond a law student or aspiring lawyer?
2. Your Writing Ability: Do you have the inherent ability to write like a lawyer?

This book focuses on the second point by giving you excellent examples of how to structure your answers. You will know exactly what to include in every sentence of your short answers to common questions relating to your motivations for law, your interest in the firm, and your skills.

The second point highlights "inherent ability", since law firms have always stressed that applicants are not expected to have legal experience. But without legal experience, you will find it difficult to understand what elite firms are looking for. This book will fill in those gaps so that you will also know how to write like a lawyer without experiencing legal work.

For the first point, I highly recommend that you pay attention to the extracurriculars your peers are focusing on and those mentioned throughout this book. You can always improve your profile by adding more diverse, impressive experiences. These experiences do not have to be related to law, debate, or politics. In fact, you can stand out simply by having other weird experiences, such as by creating the

Midnight Kayaking Society (probably does not exist, but it is definitely an eye-catching extracurricular!).

STRUCTURE: For each section of this book, there will be a brief explainer before jumping straight into the templates. There will be a sentence-by-sentence breakdown of how you can answer common questions. By reading through different successful structures, you can figure out which writing style fits your experiences and feels most natural to you.

Thanks again for your support! Let's get started.

PART I

WHY LAW

INTRODUCTION

"So, why did you choose law?"

You should have a personal, convincing answer to this question. This is important not only for your applications but also for interviews. In fact, you should have an answer memorised because you will be asked this question a lot, especially if you are also networking with lawyers and graduate recruitment.

Other variations of this question include:

- Why do you want to be a trainee solicitor?
- What are your motivations for this role?
- Why are you not applying to NON-LAW POSITION?

You should be honest, of course, but you should include elements that the law firm wants to hear. As with the rest of the book, the focus for each template is on structure to guide the content of your answer.

Before you continue reading, take a few minutes to think about why you have decided to apply to a law firm.

Be honest. Is it because of your interest in debate and legal issues? Maybe you were inspired by a family member? Perhaps it is the hefty salary? No matter what motivates you, you must twist your answer to make it sound good to graduate recruitment or practising lawyers.

While there is no right answer, at least one of your answers should relate to the training system or the work culture to show that you have pictured building a career at the firm.

Graduate recruitment also wants you to show that you understand the business of law. Show that you are interested in what commercial solicitors do.

NOTE: A major issue that students face is overlapping answers between "Why Law" and "Why You" (the next chapter). While some overlap is fine, try not to repeat your answers more than three times in your application answers and the work experience section. Think of more examples to bolster your application.

1

STANDARD TEMPLATE

Below you will find the first Why Law template. The formatting you see is how the templates will be presented throughout the book.

There will be a brief note that explains the best way to use the template, the question that the template answers, and the template itself. Every bracket represents one sentence. But since you have your own writing style, you should not be restricted by the templates. Consider the template a solid foundation for your answers.

NOTE: This template is most effective if you have at least three relevant work experiences or extracurriculars. This includes studying a law degree, vacation schemes, relevant society activities such as case study workshops, and law firm networking events that require applications.

QUESTION: Why are you interested in commercial law?

TEMPLATE:

[Introduce your interest in law by connecting it with your most highly relevant work experience or extracurricular role. If not related to commercial law, this role should have commercial elements to it.] [Link your experience with a specific skill used by lawyers to show your understanding of what a commercial lawyer does and the impact on clients. Highlight specific tasks that are relevant to the role.] [Expand on the relevance of that skill in commercial contexts and why it matters to you. This shows that you can see the bigger picture of a commercial lawyer's work and that you find that appealing.]

[Introduce the next most relevant work experience, extracurricular activity, or even any legal academic studies and link it to a commercial law career.] [Go more in-depth on one specific task in that role or a specific piece of academic work that directly links to what commercial lawyers do. Ensure that you go beyond the law and refer to the business world, economy, or commercial events.] [Introduce one more experience. Remember that non-law work experiences and extracurriculars are fine, as long as you focus on the relevant skills.] [Explain how you have spent your free time building on what you learned from that experience. This shows your proactivity and interest in commercial law.] [Conclude with a brief statement about how you can use your experiences to support clients at a commercial law firm.]

2

SHORT TEMPLATE

NOTE: This short template is less experience-heavy and focuses on delving deeper into your skills and motivations. The important part is effectively linking every skill back to why commercial law is a good fit for you.

QUESTION: Why do you want to be a commercial lawyer/solicitor?

TEMPLATE:

[Introduce your main reason for wanting to be a solicitor, such as a specific extracurricular activity or work experience. This can be non-law as long as it is business-related.] [Explain the skills you developed in relation to that main reason.] [Connect those skills to commercial lawyers to show your knowledge of the profession. For example, lawyers must have good attention to detail...] [Further link your skills to the law firm's recent deals or news. For example, reference an interesting technical deal or something you heard when networking.] [Conclude by reiterating your skills and referring to your main reason.]

. . .

[State another aspect of commercial law that appeals to you and link it to another experience.] [Highlight a specific task that relates to commercial law.] [Link the task back to why you find commercial law appealing.] [Conclude by explaining what you learned from this experience and how it will make you an effective commercial lawyer. For example, you have developed effective client relationship skills, etc.]

3

STORY-BASED TEMPLATE

NOTE: This is a more chronological, story-based template, which some graduate recruitment teams have mentioned not particularly liking. But if done well, it can also be effective. To use this template, you should be able to demonstrate how your experiences have led to a commercial law career.

QUESTION: Why do you want to be a commercial lawyer?

TEMPLATE:

[Start with a general statement about your interest in law. For example, you are curious about how the law affects the business world and society.] [Highlight your earliest relevant experience where you explored your interest. Choose something from either your last year of secondary education or during your degree.] [Show progression of your interest through another work experience. If you used an academic example before, now you can show how you sought work experience.] [End with one more experience, which can relate to academics or be an extracurricular activity. Reiterate why this interests you. For example, "After further exploring A by completing a case study at firm B, I understood that I wanted a career that…"]

[Introduce another experience. You can choose a non-law work experience or extracurricular that you invested significant time into.] [Highlight specific elements of the role that can be linked to commercial law, such as sector focus or international work.] [End with a statement that links those elements to commercial law work and reaffirms your interest. Links to law are more convincing if you can mention workshops, networking opportunities, etc.]

4

COMBINED TEMPLATE

NOTE: This is a template for firms that want you to combine "Why Law" with "Why Us". You might notice that this answer does not separate the paragraphs for the two sections of the question. Instead, the answers for both are integrated throughout the answer. This is an effective strategy if you have more legal experience. If you are lacking relevant work experience, you should try to answer "Why Law" more explicitly.

QUESTION: Explain why you want a career in commercial law and why FIRM NAME.

TEMPLATE:

[Highlight a reason you are interested in the firm. You could start with a reason related to the firm's training.] [Further explain what you know about the firm's unique training system. Is it a small intake? How many seats?] [Link the training system to an experience and explain what you enjoyed about the work or what you did well.] [Mention something unique about the firm's business. Is it strong in technology adoption? Are there notable deals?] [Explain why that element of the firm appeals to you.] [Strengthen that link to you by giving another reason that relates to training or building a career. This shows that you are thinking about committing long term to the firm.] [Summarise your two reasons and reference additional firm-specific details if needed. For example, you might say that you are optimistic about the firm's strategy.]

[Show your interest in the firm's strongest practice area. Do your research thoroughly.] [Connect that practice area with your experiences. If you do not have directly relevant experience, highlight a skill used in that sector. For example, you probably lack maritime shipping experience, but commercial awareness is a very important skill in that sector.] [Explain a task that showed that skill. Always try to quantify your achievements.] [Link that task or experience to commercial law work or clients.] [Conclude by connecting your answers to training at the firm.]

[Choose one more aspect of the firm that appeals to you. Make sure you pick a reason that you have strong experiences to back up.] [Link to work experiences, workshops, Open Days, virtual experiences, etc. Explain the specific tasks that you found enjoyable.] [If you have another extracurricular activity or experience, mention it here.] [Briefly conclude by linking your reason to working in commercial law.]

PART II

WHY YOU

INTRODUCTION

"So, why should we hire you?"

Well, your applications will not ask this explicitly. Instead, law firms ask about your skills and want you to link them to being a solicitor.

The questions that fall under this section include:

- Tell us about a time when you overcame a challenge.
- What skills have you developed that will enable your success in the role?
- In your opinion, what skills are necessary to succeed as a commercial solicitor? How have you demonstrated these skills?

Ideas of skills to include: organisational, problem-solving, teamwork, and attention to detail. While you might mention commercial awareness, it is more effective to show this skill throughout your application when discussing news, practice areas, or deals.

You should use your strongest experiences in your

application answers. Choose your most interesting and legally relevant tasks to explain how you developed your skills. The other tasks can be mentioned in your work experience section.

NOTE: If you take one thing away from this section, focus on this: For your experiences, include the hours you spent doing it, a brief description of your role, your achievements, and the impact you made. Use statistics like project budgets, percentages, and the number of team members.

1

TWO-EXPERIENCE TEMPLATE

NOTE: This template focuses mainly on two experiences. You can do this if your experiences are very relevant (ex. at a law firm) or are a substantial part of your CV (ex. you committed years doing that work or activity). If you do lack this background, you can use a similar structure but add several more experiences to bolster your answer.

QUESTION: What are two important qualities of a successful lawyer? How have you demonstrated these qualities?

TEMPLATE:

[State the first quality. In choosing the two qualities, it is a good idea to consider the qualities trainees usually have. For example, you need to be proactive, adaptable, curious, etc.] [Explain the relevance of that skill in the current legal/business landscape and to clients.] [Share a relevant experience that demonstrated the skill. Prioritise legal experiences or extracurriculars.] [Highlight a specific situation and detail how you demonstrated that skill to solve the problem.] [Emphasise how you successfully solved the problem and how you enjoyed that experience.]

[State the second quality.] [Link the quality either to the law firm's work or law firms in general. Remember that you can always reference the law firm you are applying to, even when the question is general.] [Link the quality with an experience. If you did not use a work experience in the first paragraph, you should refer to one now. Otherwise, extracurriculars or academics are fine.] [Highlight what you enjoyed about the experience, since a similar situation can occur in a law firm. For example, you might mention teamwork with international students or helping diverse customers at your part-time job.] [Bring in another experience or further elaborate on the previous one. Make sure you link back to the quality, but you can also add in new skills.] [Conclude by reiterating the importance of the second quality and how you value its importance.]

2

THREE-SKILL TEMPLATE

NOTE: For skills questions, you should aim to have three skills in your answers. This template is quite formulaic: explain the skill, expand on how solicitors use the skill, then link it to you. Having a clear structure makes your writing appear more organised and concise.

QUESTION: Explain the transferable skills you can bring to the solicitor role.

TEMPLATE:

[State the first skill. You might need two sentences to explain it.] [Explain how solicitors use that skill. For example, a solicitor must be diligent in ensuring that complex legal terms are correct to reassure clients and be an effective team member.] [Link the skill to an experience.] [Emphasise the importance of that skill for solicitors.]

[State the second skill.] [Explain how solicitors use that skill.] [Mention how that skill is useful in a general sense.

For example, communication skills are important to build friendly relationships with clients and colleagues.] [Link the skill back to a specific experience.]

[State the third skill.] [Explain how solicitors use that skill. If you feel like you are being repetitive, you can also link it to commercial law in general.] [Link it to an experience where you developed the skill.] [If you feel that your previous experience is weaker or less relevant, you can add another line with another work experience or extracurricular activity. You can use any workshops or Open Days that you have attended.]

3

DETAILED TEMPLATE

NOTE: This template is useful if you want to delve into the details of your experiences. Even if your experiences are not legally relevant, your answer will be strong if your details are memorable and convincing. To help you understand how to do this, the template breaks down every sentence used to explain the three experiences. Keep in mind the STAR framework: Situation, Task, Action, and Result.

QUESTION: What transferable skills can you bring to the role?

TEMPLATE:

[State the first skill.] [Introduce a relevant experience. You should mention at least one work experience. The others can be volunteer roles, extracurricular activities, or academic projects.] [Link the experience to the skill. Quantify your skills if possible.] [Add another point that links to the skill. This can be a problem you eventually solved or an achievement you are proud of. In the second paragraph, you will see another approach to writing about your experience.] [Explain how your skill led to success in that experience. What was the result?] [Conclude by linking your skill to the role at the law firm.]

[State the second skill.] [Link an experience to the skill.] [Identify a specific problem that occurred during the experience that required your input.] [Highlight the actions you took to solve the problem. Remember to focus on your involvement and not on what your team did. Show proactivity and creative thinking.] [Link back to how your skill will be useful in the trainee or solicitor role.]

[State the third skill. Explain how it will allow you to succeed as a trainee.] [Link to an experience and explain how you succeeded.]

4

SITUATIONAL TEMPLATE

NOTE: The key to questions that ask you to recount a situation is picking a memorable experience. Choose a situation that had urgency or required your expertise. For example, try not to focus on common problems such as tight deadlines or poor grades.

QUESTION: Tell us about a time when you were challenged and exceeded expectations.

TEMPLATE:

[State a specific situation where you were challenged.] [Explain why the situation was challenging. Be detailed to show urgency and your adaptability.]

[Explain your initial plan to tackle the problem. This shows your thoughtfulness.] [Detail how you started executing your plan.] [Provide more details on additional steps you took.] [Provide even more details. Remember that you should focus on your actions, but you can also mention reaching out to your peers and more experienced colleagues.]

[Summarise how your actions successfully handled the challenge.] [Conclude by quantifying and explaining the response to your actions. For example, use percentages to show any changes in error rates or sales growth. Mention any feedback you received from your manager or educator.]

PART III

WHY THE FIRM

INTRODUCTION

"Why do you want to join us?"

When asked about the firm, the key is to showcase your research and link it to your experiences. You should be very strategic about what you write. Think about what your background is and the types of firms that make sense. For example, do you have an international background? Do you have experience working in a niche industry? What law-related events have you attended over the years?

For your answer to be convincing, your experiences should align closely with the firm's business and culture. When you are brainstorming firms to apply to, think about which firms fit your narrative.

Other variations of this question include:

- Why are you interested in this role?
- Explain why you want to train at FIRM NAME.
- Out of the other international law firms in the City, why did you choose to apply to us?

A very effective way to improve your application is to make contact with the firm. That means having conversations with or listening to talks from trainees, associates, and partners of the firm. Attend firm events or law fairs, whether virtual or in-person. Some firms keep lists of everyone who attended and cross-reference them with submitted applications. In your answers, **specifically mention the events you attended and whom you spoke to**. Include these details naturally as you explain your interest in the firm.

NOTE: When discussing the firm's work, focus on the bread and butter practice areas. A common mistake is that students forget to research the London office specifically and instead highlight more general information that is not applicable. Some US firms keep their overseas offices small and are still building out their practices. For example, the finance practice might not be a big focus in London, but is in New York.

1

THREE-REASON TEMPLATE #1

NOTE: When answering firm motivation questions, you can mention everything, including the firm's work (ex. prominent deals) and culture. But since you are joining as a trainee, consider how training at the firm appeals to you. Think carefully about how you can link your experiences to aspects of the firm. Each paragraph in this template approaches the structure slightly differently. This template is effective if you have up to three reasons.

QUESTION: Why are you applying to FIRM NAME?

TEMPLATE:

[Briefly state your reasons for applying in one sentence. Or you can simply introduce your answer by saying, "I have three reasons for applying…"]

[State your first reason.] [Explain how you learned that information, such as at a firm event or from online research.] [Link your reason to an experience and highlight your success in that role.]

[State your second reason. It is a good idea to discuss the firm's training system or culture for newcomers as one of the reasons.] [Link your reason to the firm. Be specific to show your knowledge of the firm.] [Link what you mentioned about the firm to an experience.] [Reiterate your interest in that reason.]

[State your final reason. To sound convincing, it is helpful to reference conversations with the firm's trainees or solicitors. If you have not already, choose a reason mentioned in your interactions with the firm.] [Mention why that reason matters to you and relates to your career aspirations.] [If you have not already, you can also link your reason to the firm's recent awards and reputation.] [Conclude by linking that reason back to you again.]

2

THREE-REASON TEMPLATE #2

NOTE: Here is another template that is structured into three reasons. If you are mentioning over two reasons, you should cover different aspects of the firm. Think about the firm as a business, the clients, and your hypothetical day-to-day life as a trainee.

QUESTION: Why do you want to train at FIRM NAME?

TEMPLATE:

[State your interest in the firm's strongest practice area. You can mention the firm's ranking in London.] [Explain your interest in a prominent deal led by that practice area in the London office.] [Conclude by sharing how you researched or further explored that practice area. This can be through virtual experiences, attending a firm event, or speaking to a solicitor in that practice area.]

[Explain how the practice area differs from other competitors.] [Highlight a specific aspect of that practice area that appeals to you. Link your background to specific departments or clients that are not found in other firms. For example, some firms do not offer an art or sports practice.]

[State your second reason related to the firm's training system.] [When discussing training, refer to what you learned from networking events or firm presentations.] [Explain why the training system appeals to you.]

[Now for the final reason, you can focus on the firm's culture, commitment to ESG, etc.] [Explain what you learned from networking, your research, and workshops. You can include the names of those you spoke to.] [Link to your experience to show your interest in that reason.] [If needed, mention another experience, such as an extracurricular activity.] [Conclude by stating how the reason makes you want to train at the firm.]

3

TWO-REASON TEMPLATE

NOTE: This template uses two reasons but delves into the details within the paragraphs. The first reason is more general, and the second is very specific to the applicant's experiences. You would effectively use this structure if you have more relevant work experience.

QUESTION: Why do you want to train at FIRM NAME?

TEMPLATE:

[State your first general reason that you have ample evidence to support. For example, the firm's diversity or innovation.] [Choose a strong link to the firm, such as naming a solicitor you spoke to who inspired your reason. You should look for these opportunities through LinkedIn, law fairs, and networking opportunities.] [Explain what you learned after conducting further research to explore this reason.] [Link what you learned to the firm's clients or the market to show your strong understanding of the firm's position in the industry.] [Explain why the firm's strength in this area appeals to you.] [Support your previous sentence by referencing an experience. Relevant work experience is better than extracurriculars. However, if you are a student, as long as you have at least one work experience, you are fine.] [Link back to the firm again. Try to choose a different link than the one you chose earlier. For example, if you referenced the firm's tech deals already, mention the firm's tech seat.]

[State your second reason, such as a niche practice area which is also a strength of the firm.] [Link it to a highly relevant experience. For example, if you are drawn to the firm's strengths in supporting startups, you would mention interning at a similar firm.] [Draw on your prior experience and mention industry-specific information. Connect to the firm naturally. For example, "I want to learn how FIRM NAME supports the growth in investor interest in the German emerging companies market and…"] [Conclude by summarising why this reason appeals to you.]

4

CLASSIC TEMPLATE

NOTE: This is a safe, classic structure when answering Why Firm questions. One paragraph focuses on the firm's strongest practice area, and the other focuses on the firm's training system. To be convincing, you should conduct in-depth research to support your experiences.

QUESTION: Why are you applying to FIRM NAME over other firms?

TEMPLATE:

[Introduce two reasons for applying in one sentence. One should be related to training at the firm.]

[State the firm's strongest practice area. Do your research carefully by looking at the firm's marketing materials and the firm's London office rankings.] [Link the practice area to a relevant experience that sparked your interest in that practice area. This could be an extracurricular or academic.] [If necessary, include more information to link to your next experience.] [Introduce your second experience. This should be your strongest work experience that shows how you continued to explore this practice area.] [Explain how the experience appealed to you and link back to the firm's strength in that area.] [Reiterate your interest in the practice area.]

[State your interest in training at the firm.] [Link to a work experience, extracurricular, or academic pursuit. If your first paragraph included relevant work experience, here you can show your personality with an interesting, non-law experience.] [Mention more firm-specific details that appeal to you.] [If necessary, add another sentence on another firm-specific detail that appeals to you. This showcases all the research you did.] [Reiterate your interest in training at the firm.]

5

FIRM-SPECIFIC TEMPLATE

NOTE: When you make the effort to attend firm events, you can simply use one paragraph for every event. That makes it much easier to write a strong answer. This template is a good way to show graduate recruitment that you are very interested in the firm.

QUESTION: Explain why you are applying to FIRM NAME.

TEMPLATE:

[Introduce your interest in the firm's work, which might cover several practice areas.] [Reference an Open Day, workshop, or other event and explain what you learned. Mention any names of associates you either spoke to or heard presentations from] [Summarise what the event taught you and how it led to your application.]

[Now mention the second firm event that you attended and what you learned, perhaps about the firm's structure.

Do not repeat what you wrote for the first event.] [Mention more details about what you learned. For example, if this was an in-person event, you could explain how approachable the partners and associates were.] [Conclude by mentioning what you learned from the trainees at the event and link to why you want to train at the firm.]

[State your final reason. Aim to showcase your further research in the firm. Look at recent news on the firm's website on prominent deals, awards won, lateral hires, etc.] [Explain how the firm is uniquely strong in that area and why that appeals to you.] [Conclude by linking the reason to your career goals.]

PART IV

A NEWS EVENT

INTRODUCTION

"Tell us about a business news story that interests you."

Take your time in considering what business news to write about. Certain firms have mentioned that this answer is the first one read to get a better sense of your intellectual curiosity.

Other variations of this question include:

- Identify a current event that interested you recently.
- Tell us about a commercial event that you have been following.

In choosing a current event to write about, focus on these factors:

1. Genuine interest: If you reach the interview stage, it is very likely that you will be asked about it. So choosing a topic you care about lessens the stress of an unexpected question.
2. Challenge: Choose a topic that has unresolved

issues or challenges. Show your analytical skills by explaining it and considering solutions.

3. Legal Link: There should be some legal element to the story. For example, you might mention regulations or legal problems within your answer.
4. Recency: Even if the question does not explicitly ask you to write about a recent news event, you should still choose a story from the past year. You can link recent developments to older news.

NOTE: The way you write about a news story is up to you. But the bulk of your answer should focus on analysing the news event and explaining why you chose to write about it. You should not be merely describing the event. Rather, explain your thought process by connecting it to larger issues and industry developments.

1

STANDARD TEMPLATE

NOTE: For all the templates in this section, you will notice that the structure is more varied. You have more freedom to decide how you want to present your current news event.

QUESTION: Explain a commercial issue that interested you recently.

TEMPLATE:

[Introduce your chosen commercial issue in one sentence.]

[Highlight the main challenge or criticism related to the commercial issue.] [Explain why this commercial issue appeals to you. You do not need to link it to your background unless the question explicitly asks you to.]

[Explain the consequences and significance of the commercial issue to the stakeholders, the larger market, or the economy.] [Briefly mention any proposed solutions and potential effects.] [Link the commercial issue back to how the firm must adapt to advise its affected clients.]

[For this last paragraph, you should link the commercial issue to a less-obvious consequence. For example, if there are new strict data privacy laws, you might analyse how investors would be hesitant to invest in tech firms that handle lots of consumer data.] [Provide more details to support your analysis. You might want to reference industry reports.] [Conclude by linking back to the firm and how the firm's lawyers can help clients.]

2

STAKEHOLDER TEMPLATE

NOTE: For questions like this, you should focus on a topic related to the firm's strongest practice areas. Also, you must answer every part of the question.

QUESTION: Identify a current event that impacts the work FIRM NAME does and explain its significance to stakeholders.

TEMPLATE:

[Introduce your chosen current event.] [Provide the key details of the current event.] [Provide more details. Do not include anything that is not important to your analysis in the later paragraphs.] [Explain why you chose this topic by linking the current event to an experience. This can be an extracurricular or academic.]

[State that your current event is currently relevant to stakeholders.] [Explain the relevance to stakeholders by referencing firm performance, reputation, and sales growth.

You might mention industry reports to support your analysis.] [Reference recent news from companies that support your point. If you are applying to a law firm that mainly has UK clients, you should pick companies that are more active in the UK.] [Summarise your analysis, reiterating the significance to stakeholders.]

[State the significance and risks of the current event to the firm and the clients.] [Explain how the firm will stay updated on developments of the current event to advise clients.] [State that the firm is well-positioned to deal with the risks of the current event.] [Highlight one reason by referencing something specific to the firm. Do your research thoroughly. For example, the firm might have developed a tool to deal with similar issues or hired a particularly renowned partner.] [If you have another reason from your research, mention it.] [Conclude by reiterating that the firm will successfully handle the current event.]

3

RECENT TEMPLATE

NOTE: As emphasised in the question, choose a recent news story.

QUESTION: Choose a business news story from the past 12 months and explain why it interested you.

TEMPLATE:

[Introduce your chosen business news story. Since the question explicitly includes "past 12 months", you could include the month the story was from.] [Identify the main issue that you will later analyse.]

[Explain why the business news story appeals to you.] [Link the news to larger market or industry trends. This shows that you are intellectually curious about the bigger picture.] [Conclude by reiterating your interest in the issue.]

. . .

[State a solution to the issue. For example, if you wrote about the struggles faced by the real estate industry, you might mention new regulations implemented to lessen tax burdens for buyers.] [Link the solution to the ways law firms can support clients.] [Link to the firm specifically, either through a relevant deal or referring to the firm's practice area strengths.]

4

SHORT TEMPLATE

NOTE: Some students are unsure of how much detail they should include when discussing the current event. As you can see in this short template, every sentence contributes a different point.

QUESTION: Choose a commercial event that interests you and explain its relevance to FIRM NAME.

TEMPLATE:

[Introduce the commercial event.] [Mention researched details beyond your general topic. For example, if you chose the rise of cyberattacks, you can look for cyberattacks in specific industries and include statistical data.] [Highlight the main issue or challenge of the commercial event.] [Provide more details as necessary to provide context for your following analysis.]

[Explain the relevance of the commercial event to the firm, referring to aspects like key practice areas, prominent clients, and deals.] [Elaborate on the details in one or two sentences.] [Highlight the main uncertainties and link back to how the firm can help clients by providing tailored advice.] [Refer to the wider industry to show an understanding of the market.] [Link back to the firm's business and offerings.]

PART V

EXTRACURRICULARS, LEADERSHIP, AWARDS

INTRODUCTION

"Who are you beyond your academics?"

When faced with an extracurricular or a position of responsibility question, you should highlight a specific task or responsibility within a role in each paragraph. During your brainstorming process, think about the STAR framework to structure your responsibilities: Situation, Task, Action, and Result.

Other variations of this question include:

- Explain the responsibilities you took on outside of study and/or work.
- Detail your interests, extracurriculars, noteworthy achievements, and positions of responsibility.
- Tell us about the skills you developed from your personal experiences, extracurriculars, and positions of responsibility.

Extracurriculars can include musical instruments,

sports, time-intensive hobbies like baking or painting, and volunteering.

You must read the question carefully. Sometimes the question **DOES NOT** want you to write about work or study. For those firms, adjust your answer accordingly.

Do not spend too much time on awards, but make sure you provide enough information to show their selectiveness.

NOTE: Provide a timeframe for how much time you spend per week when introducing your work or extracurriculars. As mentioned previously, quantify your achievements if possible.

1

THREE-EXPERIENCE TEMPLATE

NOTE: This is a good template for students who lack work experience. The answer covers three experiences.

QUESTION: Tell us about your interests and extracurricular activities, including any positions of responsibility or achievements.

TEMPLATE:

[Start with your most impressive work experience or extracurricular activity that you did not already mention in your other answers.] [Introduce your specific role within that task. Even if it was a team project, focus on your own contributions.] [Provide more details and the successful result from your contributions.] [Explain what the experience ultimately taught you. Choose qualities related to working, like better collaboration and listening skills.]

[Introduce your second experience. You can mention extracurriculars, competitions, or academic essays that showcase your interests.] [Explain why you chose to do the experience, focusing on trying to learn and improve yourself.] [Provide details on how you overcame challenges during the experience.] [Summarise the successful result of your efforts and link your achievement to succeeding at the firm.]

[State your final experience. Students often choose an extracurricular here, such as a sport or a hobby.] [Explain your role and the actions you took.] [Highlight the skills you developed from the experience.] [Link these skills back to the firm and the role.]

2

TWO-EXPERIENCE TEMPLATE

NOTE: If you struggle to fill the word count with new experiences, you can focus on elaborating on what you have. This answer covers only two experiences, but you will need to pick out several situations from each experience to support your answer.

QUESTION: Please explain the key skills you've gained through work experience, positions of responsibility, personal experience, or extracurricular activities.

TEMPLATE:

[Introduce your first experience.] [State the skills you gained from a challenging situation during that experience.] [Explain the actions you took to develop that skill.] [Include another situation and explain the actions you took.] [Include one more situation.] [State that your skill led to success in that role. Quantify any metrics.]

[Introduce your second experience. When deciding on

which extracurricular to use, choose the one where you took on responsibility or held a leadership position.] [Explain the actions you took in that role and the skills you developed.] [Elaborate on the actions you took.] [Include one more situation.] [Summarise what you learned from the experience and the skills you developed to make you a better employee and colleague.] [Link your skill back to the firm.]

3

EXTRACURRICULARS TEMPLATE

NOTE: This template focuses only on extracurricular activities and hobbies, covering four experiences. You should write about hobbies that have demanded a significant amount of your time. Each paragraph is structured slightly differently, so you can choose what works for your background.

QUESTION: Please give details of any responsibilities you have taken on outside of work and/or study.

TEMPLATE:

[Introduce your first extracurricular activity. A sport is a good option, especially if it is a team sport. But anything that shows endurance and overcoming challenges is effective.] [Explain why you did this extracurricular.] [Detail the actions you took to overcome the challenges.] [Highlight one major accomplishment that you are proud of.]

[Introduce your second extracurricular activity or hobby.]

[Explain any challenges you faced or what you were responsible for.] [Mention how you handled the challenges. If you worked in a team, you can highlight your communication skills.] [Highlight your achievements, including any awards or areas of recognition.] [Summarise the skills you developed to succeed.]

[Introduce your third extracurricular activity. You can mention society activities at university, especially those related to law.] [State a specific project or activity you did. Choose something that shows your intellectual curiosity.] [Link the activity to law.] [Express your interest in skills required for solicitors, such as constructing arguments or adapting to fast-moving market changes.]

[If needed, introduce a fourth extracurricular activity.] [Explain your primary responsibilities.] [Highlight a specific skill you used. Choose one that you did not already mention.] [Link back to the skills used by solicitors to show that you are a good fit for the role.]

4

AWARDS TEMPLATE

NOTE: When prizes and scholarships are also part of the question, you might need to shorten the descriptions for every experience. In this template, there are five achievements.

QUESTION: Tell us about any prizes, scholarships, positions of responsibility, and any other noteworthy achievements that will support your application.

TEMPLATE:

[Explain your award briefly, focusing on your achievements.] [Link back to the firm's values and culture.]

[Introduce your second experience. You might choose one that showcases your teamwork skills.] [Explain the steps you took to brainstorm ideas and lead the team.] [State the skills you developed from this experience.]

. . .

[Introduce your second experience. This might be a student representative role or a leadership role in a club.] [Highlight the skills you developed.]

[Introduce your next experience. This could be less-exclusive legal experiences, such as virtual experiences or case study events.] [Outline what you learned. If you achieved a ranking during a firm event or competition, definitely mention it.]

[Introduce another experience or achievement. This can be less obvious aspects such as languages, instruments, or creative arts.] [Link the skills you developed to the firm's work.]

[Conclude by stating that your experiences align with the firm.]

PART VI

WORK EXPERIENCE

INTRODUCTION

Law firms generally want you to share your work experience in 150-word or 250-word limit answers or through a CV. For CVs, you should use bullet points and action verbs.

This section focuses on the short answers. The provided templates are separated by word count and whether it is a non-law or legal experience. As mentioned throughout this book, do not repeat the same tasks and activities you have already written about.

1

250-WORD TEMPLATES

NOTE: Here are several templates that have maximum word counts of 250 and 150 that you can follow for your work experience entries. The structure and contents of the sentences are different for each entry, so pay close attention.

QUESTION: 250-word work experience entries.

TWO TEMPLATES:

NON-LAW EXPERIENCE:

[Introduce your work or volunteer role. Remember to be specific about how many hours you worked a week.] [State the skills you developed during the experience.] [Include a specific situation when you used these skills.] [Include more details of the situation. You might need several sentences, depending on the word count.] [Mention how your actions led to a successful result.] [Link the skills you developed to a legal career.] [Link to the firm you are applying to.]

[Reiterate how you will support your colleagues and clients at the firm.]

LEGAL EXPERIENCE:

[Explain, in general terms, what you learned in the role.] [Introduce one specific task that you did throughout your experience. For example, the tasks might include drafting emails or coordinating with the team.] [Highlight the skill you developed.] [Introduce another task and explain what you learned.] [Mention how this experience helped develop your understanding of law firm work.] [Link to the firm you are applying to. Reference specific details like culture and values.] [Explain how you took advantage of networking or events to make you more certain of committing to a legal career.]

2

150-WORD TEMPLATES

QUESTION: 150-word work experience entries.

TWO TEMPLATES:

NON-LAW EXPERIENCE:

[Introduce one of your key responsibilities.] [Highlight the steps you took to fulfil your responsibility.] [Link back to the firm you are applying to. For example, you might focus on the firm's culture or values.] [Explain another skill that you developed in this role.] [Provide more details on the actions you took in developing the skill.] [Conclude by connecting the skill to legal work.]

LEGAL EXPERIENCE:

[Introduce your role.] [Provide details on your responsibilities. You can use industry lingo.] [Highlight one particular complicated task under your responsibility.] [State the skills you developed when completing the task.] [If not done already, state another skill that is highly relevant to working in a law firm. For example, you might mention interpersonal or concise writing skills.] [Link to a legal career or working at the firm you are applying to.]

COMMON-SENSE TIPS

You should not forget the basics of a good piece of writing.

Before you finish drafting your applications, here are some tips that seem very obvious but are very important to follow. When you are editing your answers and just before submitting your applications, go through this list.

1. Grammar: Does every sentence flow nicely? Have you checked your sentence in a grammar checker? One trick to check grammar is to read your answer aloud. It is much easier to notice awkward wording that way.
2. Spelling mistakes: This is an obvious problem. Your word processor should catch most of these, but double-check. Be especially careful with the firm's name and any names you mentioned. Make sure you are using British English spelling in your word processor.
3. Concise: Do not use unnecessarily long wording. Some students do this to fill the word count, but avoid providing details that do not strengthen your answers.

4. Do not be generic or cliché: You should not be writing general statements like "I am a hard worker". Show, don't tell. Brainstorm situations where you showed adversity and adaptability. Describe the actions you took and the success that resulted from that.
5. Do not repeat yourself: Always double-check that you did not repeat the same experiences over three times in your application answers and work experience section. Showing a wider variety of experiences makes you appear more well-rounded and gives a better sense of your personality. Students often downplay or forget certain achievements. This is not the time to be humble.

Addressing Common Concerns

1. Do not worry about indents.
2. Use paragraphs for application answers, but students get away with not using paragraphs for shorter work experience entries.
3. You can be slightly under the word count, but try not to be over 50 words under for application questions. Anything more means that you are likely not going in-depth enough in your answer. For work experience entries, it depends on how many responsibilities you had. If you only worked for a few months, you might only have 100 words, and that is fine.

AFTERWORD

I hope you found *The Vacation Scheme, Training Contract Applications Tiny Handbook* helpful on your legal journey!

Here's a final note: As you draft and edit your answers, remember to keep your personality. You might want to ask someone to read your application to see if it sounds like you.

And that's all! Good luck with your applications. I wish you all the success in your recruitment cycle.

If you are applying to firms that ask for cover letters, you might be interested in *The Vacation Scheme, Training Contract Cover Letter Tiny Handbook.*

ABOUT THE AUTHOR

When not thinking about the law, Leo Miles is a lover of philosophy, economics, and hot tea. Before law, he had experience in the banking sector. He enjoys quality time with his dog and reading widely.

Contact Miles through email: leomilesbooks@mail.com

www.ingramcontent.com/pod-product-compliance
Lightning Source LLC
LaVergne TN
LVHW022021200926
848481LV00007B/2469